Contents

Some things float 2

Toys that float 4

Floating and sinking games 6

Still water 8

Water flows 1 10

Water flows 2 12

Pouring water 14

Swimming 16

Air and floating 18

Large ships float 20

Sinking 22

Index 24

2

Some of these things float.

Some of these things sink.

These children are making toy boats to float.

Not all the boats are the same.
The boats are made from different materials.
Not all the boats will float well.
Some boats may sink.

What would you use to make a boat?

paper

polystyrene

Focus
float
material
sink

Some boats have been made from cement.

A log floats.

These children have thrown a log into the sea.
The log floats.
The children are throwing stones at the log.
The stones splash the water and sink.

What other things float well?

What other things sink?

Focus

float
sink

Still water has a flat surface.

This is a canal.
The water in the canal is very still.
The water has a flat surface.

What happens when you throw a stone into water?

- Focus

  still
  flat
  surface

A waterfall flows down.
It flows from the river at the top.
It flows down to the river at the bottom.

What happens to the water's surface as it flows?

Focus

surface
flow

The longest river in Britain is the river Severn. It is over two hundred and twenty miles long.

Water flows.

These children are playing in a pool.
The pool edge stops the water flowing out.
If the pool edge is pushed down the water flows out.

How would you put more water into the pool?

 Focus

flowing

The largest swimming pool in the world is as big as nine football pitches. It is in Casablanca, in Morocco.

If you tip a container water pours out.

The children are pouring water from the containers.
They are pouring water into the pool.
They are tipping containers.
The water flows out over the edge.

Do you always have to tip water out of its container?

Focus

tip
pour
container

When you swim, you float.

These children are in a swimming pool.
When people swim they float.
The water holds them up.

Why is it hard to swim underwater?

 Focus

float
swim

Penguins are birds that can swim underwater.

Air can help you to float.

This boy is learning to swim.
He needs help to swim.
He has arm bands to hold him up.
There is air trapped in the arm bands.
The air helps him to float.

What other things can help you float?

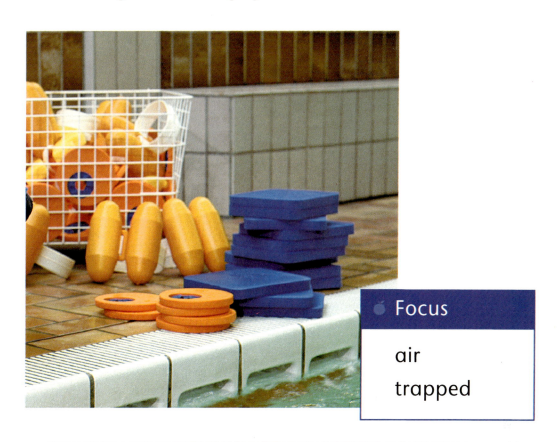

> **Focus**
>
> air
> trapped

Some large things float.

This is a large ship.
It can carry many cars.
It can carry many people.
It is very heavy but it floats well.

Have you been on a ship like this?

22

Ships float by trapping air.

Inside a ship there is a lot of air.
The air is trapped.
It is trapped by the ship's hull.
A hole in the hull will let in water.
Then the ship will sink.

Focus

trapping air
hull

Index

air   19, 23

boats   5

canal   9

floating   3, 5, 7, 17, 19, 20, 23
flowing   10, 13, 15

rivers   10, 11

sea   7
ships   20, 23
sinking   5, 7, 23
surface   9, 11
swimming   17

trapped air   19, 23

Oxford University Press, Walton Street, Oxford OX2 6DP

Oxford New York Toronto Delhi Bombay Calcutta Madras Karachi Kuala Lumpur Singapore Hong Kong Tokyo Nairobi Dar es Salaam Cape Town Melbourne Auckland Madrid and associated companies in Berlin Ibadan

Oxford is a trademark of Oxford University Press

© Nick Folkard 1993

First printed in 1993

Printed in France
by Pollina, 85400 Luçon - n° 63457L

ISBN Paperback   019 918307 4

A CIP catalogue record for this book is available from the British Library.

All rights reserved. No part of this publication may be reproduced, stored in a retrieval system, or transmitted, in any form or by any means, without prior permission in writing of Oxford University Press. Within the UK, exceptions are allowed in respect of any fair dealing for the purpose of research or private study, or criticism or review, as permitted under the Copyright, Designs and Patents Act, 1988, or in the case of reprographic reproduction in accordance with the terms and licences issued by the Copyright Licensing Agency. Enquiries concerning reproduction outside those terms and in other countries should be sent to the Rights Department, Oxford University Press, at the address above.

Acknowledgements

The publisher wishes to thank the following for permission to reproduce photographs:

Allsport /Simon Bruty p 17; Bruce Coleman /Ronald G Oulds pp 10-11; Cull Photographic pp 12, 13, 14, 15, 16, 18, 19; Chris Honeywell front cover, pp 2-3; Picthall Picture Library /Barry Picthall p 23; Tony Stone Photolibrary-London /Colin Raw pp 8-9, 20-21; Zefa /Bordis p 22.

The illustrations are by Robina Green.

Coordinating author: **Terry Jennings**
Language consultant: **Diana Bentley**
Additional contributions: **Nick Axten**
Claire Axten